EARTH'S CHANGING LANDSCAPE

Changing Coastlines

Philip Steele

First published in 2003 by Franklin Watts
Franklin Watts, 96 Leonard Street, London EC2A 4XD

Franklin Watts Australia
45–51 Huntley Street, Alexandria, NSW 2015
This edition published under license from Franklin Watts.
All rights reserved.

Series Editor: Sarah Peutrill; Series Designer: Simon Borrough; Art Director:
Jonathan Hair; Picture Researcher: Juliet Duff; Series Consultant: Steve Watts,
FRGS, Principal Lecturer in Geography Education at the University of Sunderland

Published in the United States by Smart Apple Media
1980 Lookout Drive, North Mankato, Minnesota 56003

Library of Congress Cataloging-in-Publication Data

Steele, Phillip W.
Changing coastlines / by Phillip Steele.
p. cm. — (Earth's changing landscape)
Summary: Explores the different forces that act to change Earth's coastlines,
including the effect of humans in the process and what can be done to lessen
our impact.
ISBN 1-58340-476-7
1. Coast changes—Juvenile literature. 2. Coasts—Juvenile literature. 3. Coastal
ecology—Juvenile literature. [1. Coasts. 2. Coastal ecology. 3. Ecology. 4. Nature—
Effect of human beings on.] I. Title. II. Series.

GB453.S78 2004
551.45'7—dc22   2003066195

9 8 7 6 5 4 3 2 1

Picture credits:
Corbis: 36 Michael T. Sedam; 37 Haruyoshi Yamaguchi/Corbis Sygma. James Davis
Travel Photography: 14 (bottom left), 29 (bottom), 32. Digital Vision: 8, 22, 26, 30,
33 (both), 39, 43 (bottom). Ecoscene: 15, 40 Nick Hawkes; 41 Bruce Harber; 42
Erik Schaffer. Eye Ubiquitous: endpapers and 14 (top left) A. Beszant; 13 Paul
Seheult; 19, 25 Paul Thompson; 23 C.M. Leask; 28 Nick Hanna; 34 Geoff
Redmayne; 43 (top) J.B. Pickering. Chris Fairclough Photography: 6, 10, 12, 14
(top right), 16, 35. © The Geological Society of London (www.geolsoc.org.uk)/
John Simmons: page 27 (top). Science Photo Library: 17 David Nunuk; 20
NASA; 27 (bottom) David Hardy. Still Pictures: 7 Cyril Ruoso/Bios; 11 Martin
Wright; 14 (bottom right) Jean-Louis Klein; 18 Andrew Davies; 21 Brecels &
Hodalic; 29 (top), 31 Gerard & Margi Moss; 38 Klaus Andrews.
Front Cover: David Lucas (www.dclvisions.com.au).

CONTENTS

OCEAN FRONTIERS

Many people spend time by the sea. The fresh wind, waves dragging at the pebbles, and surf pounding on the sand seem peaceful, timeless, and unchanging.

Time and tide In fact, the borders between the land and the sea are in a state of constant change. Twice daily, tides surge in over beaches and rocks and then flow back again.

Wind and waves Over the years, the action of wind and waves eats away at the land, causing cliffs to crumble and rocks to be broken down into grains of sand. This process is called **erosion**. Rivers wash tiny particles of soil, or **sediment**, out to sea. There they are caught in swirling currents and piled up into banks of mud or sand.

Great forces Even the rocks and the land are on the move. Very slowly, over millions of years, they are pushed up or folded over by the geological forces that shape Earth's surface and change its coastlines.

Beaches are changed daily by the tides coming in and out.

Coastal life Living creatures also play their part in changing the coastline. For example, corals are tiny animals encased in chalky structures that build up over the years into rock, forming reefs and islands.

Humans also alter coastlines in many ways. They build sea walls, harbors, and seaside towns. They quarry rocks from cliffs, build offshore oil rigs and pipelines, and **dredge** out channels for their shipping.

Destructive ocean

However, it is the ocean itself that is the mightiest force. It can break up piers, sink ships, or send waves crashing over houses and streets.

Massive waves batter a lighthouse.

LAND AND SEA

Water, the source of life on Earth, takes up about two-thirds of the planet's surface. Oceans such as the Atlantic and the Pacific cover vast areas. The oceans are fringed by smaller, shallower waters, such as the Gulf of Mexico, the Mediterranean, and the Baltic Sea.

Earth, as seen from space.

The land The dry land and the ocean floor are made of rock and soil. The entire Earth is a ball of rock, spinning around in space as it circles the sun.

Inside Earth the heat and pressure are intense. Some rocks are solid, some are molten. The **mantle**—a layer of hot, gooey rock—lies just below the hard outer skin of Earth, which is called the **crust**.

Earth's crust
Beneath the great **landmasses**, the crust can be up to 37 miles (60 km) thick. Beneath the oceans, the crust is only about three miles (5 km) thick. In places, the hot rock from the mantle, known as **magma**, punches its way through this thin crust. It also oozes out along gaps in the middle of the ocean floor. When it meets the cold ocean water, magma cools and hardens to form new crust, which creates underwater ridges.

Follow it through: continental drift

Earth is made up of separate plates

The plates float on the mantle

Moving apart Earth's crust is cracked, forming large sections called **plates**. These float on the mantle below and slowly shift position over millions of years.

As the landmasses move apart, new magma rises from the mantle to form ridges on the ocean floor. The movement of the landmasses is called **continental drift**. The coasts of North America and Europe are moving apart by about one and a half inches (2 to 3 cm) a year. Parts of the Pacific Rim (the countries around the Pacific Ocean) are separating at about four times that rate.

These movements may seem tiny, but over millions of years, they add up to massive distances. The world's coastlines have shifted many times during the history of the planet. About 180 million years ago, there were only two continents, called Laurasia and Gondwanaland.

Ocean depths The average depth of the oceans is about 11,500 feet (3,500 m), but can be as deep as 36,000 feet (11,000 m). Some coasts plunge into very deep ocean waters, but most slope more gently. Many landmasses are surrounded by a **continental shelf**, an underwater ledge covered in shallow seas less than 1,000 feet (300 m) deep.

Earth's landmasses have slowly drifted apart over the years, creating new coastlines for the continents.

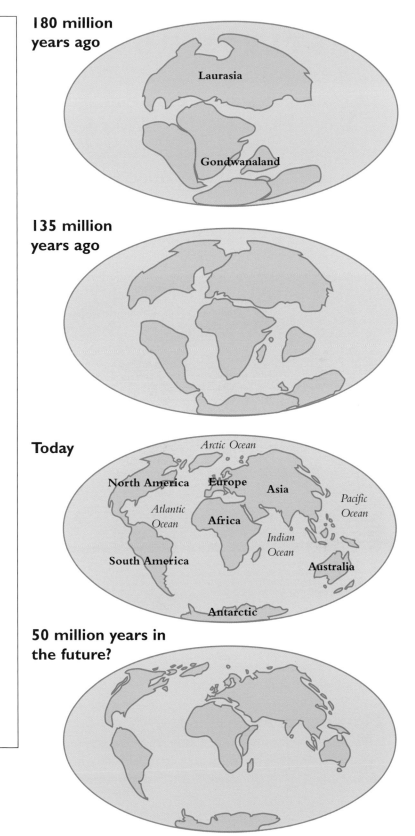

180 million years ago

Laurasia

Gondwanaland

135 million years ago

Today

Arctic Ocean

North America   Europe   Asia

Atlantic Ocean   Pacific Ocean

Africa

Indian Ocean

South America

Australia

Antarctic

50 million years in the future?

The landmasses drift very slowly

The coastlines shift position

RESTLESS ROCKS

As the plates of the crust shift and meet, they cause massive stresses and strains in Earth's rocks. Rocks are forever crushed and squeezed, heaved up, folded over, and broken by powerful forces.

Bands of coastal rock reveal geological changes over millions of years.

Turmoil Coasts are ideal places to find out more about the violent geological changes that have taken place throughout our planet's history. Here, the different bands of rock—that have been laid down over the ages—can be clearly seen, exposed in cliffs and rock faces. The bands may be folded up or down, or interrupted by a fault where an entire section of rock has slipped downward. Rocks are continually being formed, shifted, or eroded.

Flowing rocks Some rocks are created from cooling magma when existing rocks in the crust are pushed down toward the mantle and re-melted in the intense heat. Many rocks bear signs of a fiery history. Some even have tell-tale swirls that show they were once molten and flowed over the ground.

Follow it through: raised beaches

Wave action along a coastline forms a beach and cliffs

Coastal land is lifted up by rock movements

Building up Other rocks are **sedimentary**. These are created by the build-up of sediment—such as broken seashells on ocean floors—that is later pressed into hard slabs. Examples include limestone, sandstone, and shale.

Fossil evidence Fossils show us how living creatures and natural habitats have changed over the ages. They are often found in sedimentary rocks, and may include corals, fish bones, starfish, sea urchins, worms, and the impressions or molds of seashells. Some of the most interesting marine fossils are of creatures which no longer exist. These include ammonites—spiral-shelled creatures which lived about 100 million years ago—and trilobites, which were crawling over ocean floors about 500 million years ago.

Take it further
Look at some different sorts of fossils by:

◆ Visiting a coast. You may find some fossils in stones or boulders lying on the beach.
◆ Visiting a museum with a natural history collection.
◆ Researching fossils in a book or on the Internet.
◆ Can you identify the different sorts of creatures?

Moving rocks Movements inside Earth, or the melting of heavy layers of ice, can both cause sections of coast to be heaved up above sea level, forming **raised beaches**. Over millions of years of upheaval, coastal rocks can even be thrust to the top of an inland mountain range. Fossils of prehistoric sea creatures, whose remains or imprints have become hardened in the rock, can be found far from today's coastlines.

The Seven Sisters cliffs on the Sussex coast in the UK are made up of the remains of millions of tiny sea creatures.

The sea level drops and forms a new, lower shore

The old coastline is left high and dry as a raised beach

The pull of the moon's gravity is the most powerful force that creates tides.

Tides, ocean currents, winds, and waves all affect the conditions along our seashores. To understand how they work, we need to study Earth in space and its position in relation to the sun and moon.

Tides Stars, planets, and moons all pull things toward them. This tugging force is called gravity. Earth is affected by the gravity of the sun and the moon. Each day, the moon causes the nearest oceans on Earth to bulge outward, causing a tide.

The spinning motion of Earth means that oceans on the other side of the world also rise and fall with the tide. When both the sun and moon line up to pull in the same direction, we experience the highest tides of the year.

Ocean currents The heat of the sun warms the upper waters of the oceans, but the lower waters remain bitterly cold. There is also a geographical difference. The sun shines most directly on the oceans around the equator, which become very warm. It shines much less directly on Earth's polar regions, where the waters stay very cold.

Cold water is denser than warm water. It sinks, and warmer surface water rushes in to take its place. These swirling movements build up into powerful currents around the world's oceans. Currents are like great oceanic rivers shifting up to 50 million tons of water per second. They have a great effect on the weather and climate of coastal regions and on the coastline.

Follow it through: wave movement

Within a wave, the water moves around in circles

As the wave meets a shelving coast, the circles become flattened into an oval shape

Winds The difference in temperature between the equator and the poles also affects the air around Earth. As warm air rises, cooler air moves in to take its place, creating patterns of winds. The direction of these winds is angled by Earth's spin.

Local temperature differences also create winds. During the day, the land warms up more quickly than the sea. The air above the land becomes warmer and rises, and cooler air from above the sea moves in to replace it, creating a sea breeze. During the night the land cools more quickly than the sea, and so a breeze blows from land to sea. All of this affects the local coastal weather, and in turn, the vegetation that grows there.

The way in which waves break is affected by the obstacles they meet on the shore.

Waves Winds are the chief movers of waves. The surface waters are forced away from the advancing wind at an angle. This movement sets off whirling movements in deeper waters, which build up to an ocean swell. The biggest waves may measure over 100 feet (30 m) from trough to crest.

The wave now loses some of its force and begins to slow down

As new waves pile in from behind, the crests of the waves become closer together

The waves break as surf

PEBBLES, SHINGLE, AND SAND

Each beach, or part of a beach, has its own mixture of stones or sand, created by the force of the waves.

Round pebbles

Shingle beach

Shell beach

Sandy beach

Sheer cliffs may plunge directly into the ocean, but most coasts slope gradually and are bordered by beaches. As the waves power their way in from the ocean, they may break up fragments of rock or shell into banks of loosely-packed shingle.

Boulders and stones

Waves rub boulders and pebbles against each other until they are round and polished smooth. Waves then dump the heavier boulders at the lower levels of the beach, while small pebbles are carried further by the surf.

Sand and water
Over time, waves can grind even the hardest stone—such as granite or basalt—into sand, forming billions of tiny grains. The sand itself is part of the process of erosion, for it also rubs away at pebbles and shells.

Over millions of years, stony beaches may turn into sandy ones. Sandy beaches might in turn become covered in stones or shingle again, as a result of a storm or a rockfall.

**Follow it through:
from stone to sand**

Waves crash
onto the beach

Friction of the waves
erodes stones

Sand and wind Along the top of some beaches, the sand stays dry except during storms. It is easily stirred up into flurries by the wind. Fierce winds may sand-blast rocks and cliffs, causing severe erosion. Along open beaches, sand may be piled up into dunes by the wind. These soft banks are constantly on the move, often advancing into land far behind the beach.

Unless grasses root in sand dunes and hold them firm, the dunes shift with the wind.

Take it further

There are hundreds of different types of rock and stone. Collect some samples and use a guide book to identify them.

◆ Compare their colors and structure. Do they contain any glittering crystals? Are they dull or shiny?
◆ Try scratching them. Are they very hard? Or are they soft and crumbly?
◆ Leave them in a bucket of water. Do they soak up water? Do they dissolve easily? Which ones do you think will erode most rapidly?

Over millions of years, rocks become sand

Sand in the water erodes pebbles and shells

Wind-blown sand erodes cliffs and rocks

LIVING SHORES

The seashore is one of the most changeable of all **habitats**—or living places—for plants and animals. Most habitats change slowly with the seasons, but the seashore is flooded by saltwater tides twice daily, pounded by the surf, and swept by strong winds. However, the seashore is rich in life-supporting oxygen, water, and minerals which support many plants and small animals. These, in turn, provide a meal for other creatures.

The recent high water mark on any beach is normally easy to spot, for it is often marked by a long line of seaweed or driftwood, which has been washed up and left behind by the tide.

The upper shore At the top of a sandy or rocky shore is an area called the "splash zone." This is never covered by water, but may be spattered by wind-blown spray and foam. Little creatures such as sea slaters or sandhoppers may be seen scurrying around. Large areas of the upper shore may be covered with water only during storms or the highest tides.

Starfish like to live in shallow waters, such as this rockpool.

Take it further

Make a list of the things you would expect to find in a rockpool.

◆ If you can, check your answer by exploring a rockpool at low tide. Remember to beware of slippery rocks and the incoming tide. Lift stones and examine animals or plants in a bucket of seawater, but always put them back again.
◆ If you don't live near the sea, use reference books or the Internet.

Mid and lower shores

The middle and lower regions of the shore are covered and uncovered with every tide. Much of the wildlife is hidden under the sand or boulders. This is the home of shore crabs, worms, whelks, winkles, shrimps, and seaweeds.

As the tide goes out it leaves behind pools of seawater in the rocks. For about 12 hours, each tidal pool is a world in itself until the surf crashes over it once again.

Below the low tide limit, the area is always covered by water. Here are tangles of seaweed, starfish, sea urchins, small fish, crabs, lobsters, and octopus.

COASTAL EROSION

All coastlines are eroded by the force of the wind and waves. The friction is increased by the movement of sand and pebbles.

Under pressure

Seawater forces its way into holes, cracks, and fissures in the rock. The air in these spaces is placed under massive pressure, as much as 65 tons per square inch (10 tons per sq cm). It is no wonder that over the years joints in the rock begin to split open, causing sections of the cliff to tumble into the ocean.

Cracks and crumbles

Waves carrying pebbles can grind down rocks and eat away entire coastlines. Winds blast rocks with sand and grit, carving them into strange shapes. Heat from the sun can make rocks swell, or expand, and crack. Moisture inside porous rocks may turn into ice. This takes up more space and forces the rock to crumble. Layers of soft rocks erode quickly, while hard rocks survive longer.

Powerful waves have pounded and sucked this crumbling cliff, clawing out deep caves along the coastline.

Follow it through: coastal erosion

Waves erode the soft rock on a cliff

A hard section of the cliff survives, forming a headland

Waves eat through softer sections of the headland

Shaping the coastline

Sea caves and **blowholes** are carved out by erosion. Erosion also shapes capes, bays, and coves. It bores arches through headlands, which then collapse to form offshore pillars, called **stacks**. Waves claw out the bases of cliffs and stacks, causing them to collapse. The waves may cut out a wide platform of rock at the foot of cliffs. Platforms, ledges, and reefs protect surviving cliffs from further erosion by breaking the force of the waves.

Case study: London Bridge, Australia

London Bridge was a headland on the coast of Victoria in Australia. Rolling ocean breakers had created natural arches in its rocks. In January, 1990, the arch nearest to the main coastline suddenly collapsed into the sea. Two people were stranded on the end of the headland, which is now an island. They had to be rescued by helicopter.

London Bridge, Australia: one arch down, one to go.

A natural arch is created, which later collapses into the sea

A small island is left and is further eroded

Eventually only a rocky pillar remains

Erosion levels the coast to a platform of rock extending from the shore

SEDIMENT AND SILT

Coastlines are not frontiers just between land and ocean, but also between freshwater rivers and the salty sea. **Estuaries**, the areas where rivers meet the sea, are affected by tides. Many are bordered by **salt marshes** and banks of mud and sand. These areas are forever slipping, sliding, and oozing.

Rivers and deltas Rivers carry huge amounts of sediment out to estuaries and nearby coasts. This may build up into a slope at the mouth of the river, until the main watercourse becomes clogged with **silt**. The river is then forced to split into separate channels as it finds its way to the sea. Such coasts, called **deltas**, may extend the coastline by many miles over the centuries.

Advancing coastlines Sediment can also build new coastlines by piling up into sandbanks and spits. These strips of land often create calm coastal pools called **lagoons**, and serve as a barrier against the full force of the waves. The lagoons may eventually silt up completely. Once a new coastline has been created, it will in turn be eroded by incoming waves.

The Mississippi delta region covers an area of more than 12,000 square miles (32,000 sq km). This colored satellite image shows the land in light blue, water in dark blue, and sediment in green.

Case study: Mississippi River

The Mississippi River drains a vast area of the U.S. Its waters are thick with mud that is washed downstream by spring rains. This sediment amounts to about 360 million tons (330 million t) each year.

Advancing into the sea

Around the mouth of the river, the mud has built up into a marshy delta with many different channels. These empty into the Gulf of Mexico, a shallow sea without any big tides or strong currents to flush away the sediment. For that reason, the coastline advances into the sea by about two-thirds of a mile (1 km) every ten years.

Follow it through: lagoon creation

Ocean currents dump sediment offshore

Over the years, the sediment piles up into a long sandbank, or bar

As the bar grows in size, it makes waves break offshore

Mangrove swamps build up tropical coasts and provide a barrier that protects the land against floods and storms.

Plants and animals

The building up of coastal sediment is called **accretion**. Both plants and animals may help the process along. In tropical regions, the tangled roots of mangrove trees trap mud and sand, extending the coastline each year.

On rocky coasts in South America, seabirds leave many droppings, called "guano." Over the centuries, this may build up and harden into thick layers, weighing many tons.

The bar grows to enclose quiet, inshore waters as a lagoon

The lagoon fills up with sediment and becomes land

The seabed is now deeper and waves erode the new coast

ICE BOUND

Some of the most severe coastal changes occur in the Arctic and Antarctic, where coasts may be gripped and ground out by thick ice. Some of this is a permanent ice sheet, which remains frozen hard all year round.

Adelie penguins and Leopard seals rest on Antarctic ice floes.

Ringed with ice The North Pole lies in the middle of the frozen Arctic Ocean. The South Pole is on the Antarctic landmass, where the ice can reach a depth of nearly three miles (5 km) in places. Antarctic coasts are ringed with ice. In some places, glaciers—frozen rivers—meet up to form broad ice shelves around the coast.

Around the permanent ice are regions where the ice breaks up or melts during the brief polar summers. In autumn, as the weather becomes cold again, floating slush and blocks of ice lock together into drifting masses of **pack ice**.

Follow it through: icebergs

Snow falls and builds up on Arctic mountains

The snow is compressed to form heavy ice

The ice slips downward toward the coast

Icebergs Large blocks of ice called "icebergs" regularly break away from polar coasts and drift out to sea. Chunky Arctic icebergs are formed mostly in Greenland, where about 15,000 are "calved" from coastal glaciers each year. This means that end sections of glaciers break off into the ocean. These may be almost a mile in length, but 90 percent of their bulk remains underwater.

Antarctic icebergs mostly break away from the ice shelves. They are flat and ride a bit higher in the water. These are real giants. Some have a recorded size of 11,500 square miles (30,000 sq km)—an area about the same size as Belgium!

A slab-shaped iceberg drifts among smaller ice floes during the Antarctic summer.

Take it further
Freshwater found in ponds and lakes freezes at 32°F (0°C). However, the temperature has to drop below 28°F (−2°C) before seawater freezes over. Even then, only the coastal fringes are likely to be icy. It takes really severe weather conditions for the open sea to turn to ice.

◆ Seawater has a lower freezing point than freshwater because it contains salt. Test this by placing two ice-cube trays in the freezer compartment of a refrigerator. One should contain tap water. The other should contain water mixed with salt. Which one freezes first? Keep checking the trays about every 30 minutes.

The ice is channeled into slow-moving glaciers that flow to the coast

End sections are weakened by the action of the sea

Great blocks of ice crash into the sea and the new iceberg drifts through the ocean

DROWNED COASTS

The planet Earth does not have a constant climate. In its history there have been many Ice Ages. These were periods of great cold, interrupted by occasional warmer periods. A major Ice Age began about 600,000 years ago.

High and low During the coldest periods of the Ice Age, the polar ice sheets reached far beyond their present range. A large amount of Earth's water remained locked in these frozen masses, which meant that sea levels were very low.

About 11,000 years ago, the climate became warmer again. In the thousands of years that followed, large amounts of water were released from the ice sheets.

Great floods As the polar ice melted, sea levels began to rise around the world. Low-lying islands and coastal plains were flooded. Areas of high ground became islands. Seas spilled over the land, creating new channels and straits.

Case study: North Sea coasts

If a map had been drawn of North Sea coasts about 11,000 years ago, it would have shown much more land than today. A great band of low-lying land covered the southern half of the sea, joining Great Britain with France, Belgium, the Netherlands, and Denmark. The river Thames flowed into the Rhine. The Dogger Bank, an area of sandbank and shallows in the North Sea, was a large island.

The rising sea
As sea levels rose after the big freeze, water flooded in to create the present coastlines. The North Sea was now linked to the English Channel, making Great Britain an island. Parts of the east coast of Great Britain and the north coast of the Netherlands became low-lying wetlands, regularly flooded by the sea.

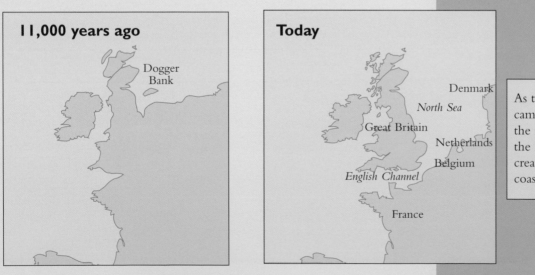

11,000 years ago

Dogger Bank

Today

Denmark
North Sea
Great Britain
Netherlands
Belgium
English Channel
France

As the last Ice Age came to an end, the rising levels of the North Sea created new coastlines.

Follow it through: rising sea

Earth's climate gets warmer

Polar ice sheets melt

Sea levels rise

The coastline of Norway was created when the ocean flooded into valleys left behind by glaciers.

Fjords Where glaciers had ground out deep valleys, the sea rushed in to create deep-sea inlets called **fjords**. Many of the world's most familiar coastlines took on their present shapes during these floods. Climate change will one day cause such dramatic changes again.

Take it further

All over the world there are ancient tales and stories about great floods and lands lost beneath the waves. They appear in the Bible, in many other ancient scriptures, and in folk tales.

◆ Could they be distant memories of real floods, passed down from one generation to the next? Investigate a famous flood story such as the one found in the Bible.

Low-lying islands and plains flood

Areas of high ground become islands

New channels, straits, and fjords are created

FIRE FROM THE SEA

Coasts and islands that experience the most violent changes are volcanic. They are created when molten magma bursts through Earth's crust in the form of **lava**. Many volcanoes are located around the edges of plates (*see page 9*), such as the South Atlantic island of Tristan da Cunha. Others, such as the Hawaiian islands, are located above **hotspots** in the middle of plates.

Out of the depths Eruptions of lava may build up into massive underwater volcanoes. The cooled and hardened lava forms cones that eventually break the surface of the ocean as islands. Sometimes lava simply oozes out through the crust in a gooey, red-hot flood, and forms islands without a big eruption.

A volcano may remain active for thousands of years. As more and more lava is poured into the waves, it builds up new rocks and reefs around the coastline. These are eroded by wave action. Lava may be ground down into black or gray sand.

An eruption and lava flow of the Kilauea volcano on the island of Hawaii. Kilauea volcano is one of the most active volcanoes in the world, with many eruptions and flowing lava lakes that alter the coastline around it.

Follow it through: volcanic islands

Molten magma bursts through the ocean floor

Red hot lava cools and hardens on contact with the seawater

With each new eruption, the mass of hardened lava grows higher

The volcanic island of Surtsey today.

Case study: Surtsey, Iceland

In November 1963, hot magma oozed from the seabed off the coast of Iceland. Cold seawater turned to steam instantly in a series of massive explosions. A great plume of smoke and ash rose high into the air.

Rising from the sea

Over the next three years, a new island of black lava arose from the waves. It soon covered an area larger than a square mile (3 sq km) and was named Surtsey, meaning Surt's Island. In the old tales of the Vikings, Surt had been a fiery giant.

A big blast Volcanoes may also destroy the islands they have created. Really big eruptions have the power to blow a whole island out of the water. Krakatoa, in Indonesia, was blasted sky-high in 1883, leaving an ocean-filled crater where once there had been dry land. Volcanic islands may also be destroyed when the hollow crater at their center collapses inward.

Giant waves Underwater eruptions and earthquakes send out powerful shock waves. These travel across the ocean floor at high speeds, whipping up a massive wave called a "tsunami." When this meets a shelving coastline, it rises up with devastating effect. The wave triggered by the eruption of Krakatoa killed 36,380 people.

Before the volcano blast.

The island today.

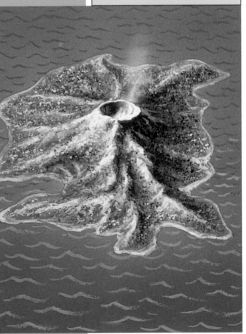

The coastline of Thíra (also known as Santorini), a Greek island, was created about 3,500 years ago. A massive volcanic eruption blew out the center of the island.

The volcanic rock breaks the surface and forms an island

New eruptions increase the size of the island

A massive eruption blows the island apart, leaving only scattered remnants of land

CORAL KINGDOMS

There are many types of coral. Species known as "true" or "stony" corals are tiny creatures that live on the seabed in large groups called colonies. Their soft bodies are protected by hard, chalky structures. These build up into rocky masses, which survive even after the creatures have died. They form beautiful **reefs** and islands in tropical seas. Corals thrive only in warm, clear water, and die if buried in sediment.

Coral reefs grow in warm, clear waters. They attract all kinds of sea animals and plants, and are fascinating to explore.

Follow it through:
atoll formation

A volcanic island builds up in tropical waters with coral growing outward from its shores

The coral forms a rocky platform

Coastal reefs and atolls

Fringing reefs grow outward from a coastline, forming a submerged platform of coral rock.

Many such reefs build up around volcanic islands. If these later collapse into the ocean, the corals continue to grow in the ring shape of the former coastline. These circular reefs are called **atolls** and enclose a calm lagoon.

Offshore reefs

Barrier reefs lie away from the coast. Many originally bordered coastlines that later sunk because of geological upheaval, or were drowned by rising sea levels. Barrier reefs protect a coastline against the waves of the open ocean, taking the full force of tropical storms. They are pounded and eroded by waves.

Maria atoll, in French Polynesia, forms a typical coral ring in the South Pacific.

Case study: The Great Barrier Reef, Australia

The world's longest stretch of coral, the Great Barrier Reef, runs parallel to the coast of eastern Australia for 1,257 miles (2,027 km). It is made up of about 350 different coral species. The outer part of the reef was formed millions of years ago. The inner reef and coastal islands are part of a coastline that was drowned by the sea in prehistoric times.

The Great Barrier Reef extends southward from the Coral Sea, parallel to the coast of Queensland, Australia.

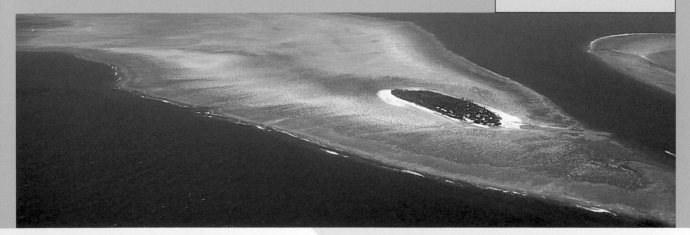

As the island begins to collapse and sink, the coral—now separated by sea from the remaining island—forms a barrier reef

Eventually the center of the island also sinks into the water and disappears, leaving a ring of living coral that forms an atoll

THE HUMAN FACTOR

Coasts have been settled by humans since prehistoric times. Early peoples came to the shoreline to gather shellfish, and to spear or net fish. They soon learned to make canoes and ships, and to start trading. Today, many coastlines and banks of estuaries have become completely built up with fishing harbors, seaports, towns, or big cities. Many industries—such as shipyards, docks, oil refineries, and tourist resorts—need to be located on a waterfront.

The natural shoreline of Cape Town, South Africa, has been transformed by docks, harbors, and buildings.

Diggers and bulldozers Human activities may change coastlines forever. People dredge out channels for shipping. They drain marshes for building or farming. They cut down forests, resulting in more and more soil being washed into rivers. Much of this sediment is then flushed out to sea. Humans mine for coal, tin, or phosphates in coastal regions and quarry cliffs for their stone. They place rigs offshore to drill for oil and natural gas under the seabed. They build structures such as roads, bridges, tunnels, quays, and piers.

Case study:
Oil on the Bay of Biscay

The Bay of Biscay is a section of the Atlantic Ocean that stretches from northwestern France to northern Spain. It is home to dolphins, squid, tuna, whales, and all kinds of seabirds.

Tanker disaster

Biscay is famous for its rocky coasts, storms, and rough seas. It is also famous for shipwrecks—and frequent oil spillage. The *Prestige* was an oil tanker that sank there on November 19, 2002. It had 60,000 tons of heavy fuel oil on board. Soon the stinking, tarry fuel was washing up on Spanish coasts. Tens of thousands of seabirds were coated in oil. Tourist beaches were ruined. Fishing boats could not leave port.

Cleaning up

Research has shown that heavy fuel traces remain in the coastal sediment almost indefinitely. Methods of cleaning up oils spills have improved over the years, but the disasters still need to be prevented. Tanker construction, shipping routes, and inspection of vessels need to be more carefully controlled.

Oil spillages wreak havoc along coastlines, particularly to wildlife.

Take it further
Choose three different coastal settlements and look at them on detailed maps.

◆ What are the main features and land uses for each one?
◆ What do you think are the reasons for any differences?

Human threats Many human activities disrupt, destroy, or pollute coastal habitats. Big trawlers overfish sea areas until stocks run out. People strip tropical islands of their mangrove, or break up coral to make tourist souvenirs and building material. Sewage is piped out to sea, and garbage or hazardous waste is dumped into the oceans. River estuaries and coastal waters may be poisoned by factory waste or chemical fertilizers washed from farmland.

Protecting the environment Human damage to the world's coasts can be limited. Some estuaries that were polluted and filthy 50 years ago are now clean and teeming with fish. With good scientific research, strict laws, and careful management, coastal habitats and their wildlife can be rescued, restored, and protected. However, making our coasts cleaner depends on governments being prepared to spend money, and on international laws being passed and enforced.

Overfishing in the North Sea threatens fish stocks.

COASTAL DEFENSES

These groynes protect a sandy shore from erosion.

The changing conditions along coastlines often make life difficult for humans. Natural processes such as erosion may place buildings or valuable farmland in danger. Silting can block ports and shipping channels. Storms can destroy entire communities. People try to control this unpredictable environment, and protect themselves from the wind and waves.

Stopping erosion

Breakwaters are barriers of rock, stone quays, or timber jetties designed to break the force of the waves as they approach a shore. **Groynes** are barriers of wood or stone built out from the shore. They slow down strong currents and trap sediment which might otherwise be swept away.

Shores may be planted with tough plants such as marram grass, so that roots will stabilize shifting sands. **Conservation** of mangrove prevents coastal erosion of tropical islands.

Storm defenses Sea walls, dams, and dikes are built to prevent coastal flooding. Storm barriers may be constructed to protect cities from flooding. A severe hurricane struck the city of Galveston, Texas, in 1900, killing about 6,000 people and nearly destroying the city. After that, a massive sea wall was built to protect the city from further waves and flooding.

Sea walls and barriers are very expensive to build and maintain. It may be impossible to protect an entire coast against rising sea levels or large-scale erosion. Nature's own defenses are sometimes the best. One costly plan to build a sea wall at Essex, UK, was abandoned when it was realized that allowing a natural salt marsh to develop could provide an effective— and free—defense against flooding.

The Delta Project in the Netherlands is an incredible feat of engineering.

Case study: The Delta Project, the Netherlands

In 1953, tides and storms caused massive flooding of the low-lying lands around the North Sea. Almost 2,000 people were killed in the Netherlands alone.

Building a defense
From 1958 to 1996, engineers attempted to stop this from ever happening again by building a vast system of defenses along the coast of Zeeland, in the Netherlands, sealing off the mouths of the Maas, Rhine, and Scheldt rivers.

The East Scheldt River has a barrier six miles (9 km) long, with 62 steel gates. When these are open the tide can flow freely in and out of the estuary. When danger threatens, they are raised.

NEW LAND FROM THE SEA

Land is very precious to humans, and they have learned how to **reclaim** it from the sea or to build artificial offshore islands. The new land may be used for farming, for building new towns, or as a safe site for an airport.

Having already built upward with skyscrapers, the tiny country of Monaco is forced to build outward into the sea for further development.

Greenfield sites In order to reclaim land, seas must be sealed off by dikes or dams, then drained and filled with soil.

Over the last 600 years, the Dutch have perfected this process. More than 40 percent of the Netherlands is now reclaimed land, or **polder**. Much of the new land was once part of the Zuyder Zee. In 1932, this shallow sea was contained by a 20-mile (32-km) Afsluitdijk, or "barrier dike." It became a vast freshwater lake, renamed as the Ijsselmeer. Since then, much of the lake has been converted into polder, section by section. Where the waves once rolled in, herds of cows now graze flat, green farmland, and cars drive through the streets of new towns.

Growing cities Some crowded cities have little space to grow, and so expand into the sea. Monaco, the world's second smallest country, is only .6 square miles (1.6 sq km) in area. Its territory, surrounded by France, borders the Mediterranean Sea. Monaco is entirely built up, so any land for further development must be taken from the sea. Land reclamation along this coast threatens the survival of coral species.

Follow it through: land reclamation

An area of shallow seabed is sectioned off with watertight dams

The seawater is slowly pumped out from the enclosed area

Airports Big airports are sometimes located offshore. These may be natural islands or they may be artificial platforms built up from the seabed. These locations reduce the risk of air disasters taking place over centers of population, and remove aircraft noise and pollution from city suburbs. Kansai Airport is built on a 1,260-acre (510-ha) artificial island in Osaka Bay, Japan. By 2007, it will have doubled in size.

Take it further
The shores of reclaimed land or artificial islands experience the same attack from winds and waves as do natural shores.

◆ How might they be prevented from becoming swamps?
◆ How might they be protected from flooding?
◆ How might they be protected from erosion?

Japan's Kansai airport is built on huge platforms of concrete, which form a new island in Osaka Bay.

The empty area is filled in with rocks, soil, and sand while grasses, trees, and other plants stabilize the soil

The new coastline is protected with strong dikes

Roads, farms, villages, and towns may be built on the reclaimed land

CLIMATE CHANGE

Changes in the world's climate are not new. Past Ice Ages have shown how the world may slowly become colder or warmer over tens of thousands of years. In recent years, many scientists have argued that the world's climate is warming much more rapidly than before. If **global warming** continues, it could have a great impact on sea levels and coastlines.

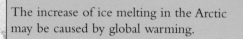

The increase of ice melting in the Arctic may be caused by global warming.

The global hothouse

Traffic exhaust, factory smoke, burning forests, and farming activities create gases such as carbon dioxide, nitrous oxide, and methane. These form a layer in Earth's **atmosphere**. The gases act as a barrier that prevents heat from escaping. The planet's landmasses and oceans start to become warmer.

Not all scientists agree about the extent of global warming, its timescale, or its importance. However, a rise in the average temperature of only 1°F (0.5°C) has widespread effects. There is clear evidence that Antarctic ice shelves are breaking up, Arctic wildlife is suffering from temperature change, and weather patterns in many parts of the world appear to be less settled.

Follow it through: global warming

Cars, planes, and power plants burn "fossil fuels" (oil, coal, natural gas) full of carbon dioxide

Methane gas is released by cattle ranching, coal mining, and rice farming

Nitrous oxide is emitted by forest fires, cement factories, and fuels

Coasts at risk

Further melting of the polar ice sheets would cause a rise in sea levels around the world, as at the end of the last Ice Age (*see page 24*). This would threaten low-lying coasts and regions such as the Nile Delta in Egypt. Famous cities on the existing waterline, such as Venice, Italy, could also sink beneath the waves. Island chains such as the Maldives or the Florida Keys could vanish altogether.

If seawater enters the freshwater table of an island, it makes springs and wells undrinkable. No island can survive without drinking water. Hundreds of millions of people could be made homeless, and vast amounts would need to be spent on new coastal defenses.

Stormy weather

Climate change could make many coasts stormier. Hurricanes could become more violent. Major changes in ocean temperature could also alter the course of ocean currents, making some coasts colder than they are now. Fisheries could collapse as certain fish species fail to breed.

Bangladesh already suffers from extreme flooding. Rising sea levels could be disastrous for the country's huge population.

Take it further

Find out more about climate change. Collect newspaper articles and reports. Search the Internet. For example, look at www.epa.gov/globalwarming/kids. Watch for related radio and TV programs.

◆ What are the scientists' worst fears?
◆ What are people doing to prevent climate change?
◆ What do oil companies say about the problem?
◆ What do campaigning groups such as Greenpeace propose?

| Gases form a layer around Earth that sunlight can pass through | Some of the warmth rising from Earth passes through the layer, but the rest is reflected back to the surface | Earth's temperature rises relatively rapidly, melting the polar ice sheets | Coastlines are altered |

WIND AND WAVE POWER

Power plants which generate electricity are often located on sea coasts and estuaries, where there is a constant supply of water for use as a coolant. Power plants that are fired by coal, natural gas, or oil may pollute the air and contribute to global warming. Nuclear power plants carry their own risks, such as the release of dangerous radioactive material into the environment.

The Rance estuary tidal barrage in Brittany, France, also serves as a road bridge.

Safer energy Coastal regions have their own natural energy—sunshine, winds, tides, and waves. All of these can be harnessed to generate the electricity we need for our homes and industries. These sources of power are clean and safe. They are currently operated on a small scale and may be expensive. They need to be developed—and their use greatly extended—if they are to become affordable and play a larger part in energy production.

Barrages Turbines which produce electricity can be driven by the force of tides passing through a **barrage** built across an estuary.

Like all coastal constructions, barrages across estuaries can cause problems to the environment and the local plants and wildlife. Construction may create new jobs, but threaten other traditional industries such as fisheries or mussel beds.

Follow it through: coastal barrages

Clean, renewable energy is needed

Barrages are built to harness wave power

Investigate **renewable energy**.

◆ How much of your country's energy need is met by renewable energy sources?
◆ What is the government's policy on renewable energy, especially tidal power?

Offshore tanks One alternative to the estuary barrage is to create huge tanks offshore on the seabed. These tidal basins fill and empty with the tides, driving turbines.

Floats and turbines Other alternative methods include anchoring arrays of floats offshore to pick up wave motion and convert it into power. Wind turbines can be set up along windy coasts, or built offshore on reefs or platforms.

Careful planning can overcome most problems. The great advantages to the environment are that these sources of energy are clean and safe—they don't produce carbon dioxide, and unlike oil, coal, or natural gas, they are endlessly renewable.

Wind turbines on the coast of Denmark produce clean, renewable power.

Tidal waters are altered

Channels silt up

Plants and animals are affected by an environmental change

Some animals, such as salmon, may not be able to migrate

COASTAL FUTURES

Humans need to live in coastal regions and make use of them in many different ways, as they have done throughout history. Our shores and coastal waters are a precious resource, and their future needs to be safeguarded. This means we need to both live in harmony with nature, and protect coastlines from ourselves.

Coastal erosion has caused this building to fall off the cliff. Many buildings on coasts are threatened by the erosion of cliffs.

Follow it through: tourism

Beautiful beaches

Coastal tourist development

Workers clear beached oil from a grounded tanker.

Take it further:
Investigate an environmental issue in a coastal area, such as the building of a new yachting marina or tidal barrage.

◆ Find out as much as you can about it. What positive and negative effects will it have?
◆ Do the local people generally support or oppose the project?

Living in harmony Humans are no match for the awesome powers of nature. We may be able to take back a bit of land from the sea here or there, but we cannot stop the endless process of erosion, or prevent a volcano from blowing an island apart. We must work out ways to live in harmony with nature, rather than seeking to control or oppose it.

In practical terms, that means conserving, planning, and managing the environment. It means countries around the world working together, putting laws in place, and enforcing them. This may be difficult because there will always be people who wish to make money regardless of damage to the planet.

Accident prevention Oil spills or pollution are not natural events, and can be prevented. They are not just bad for the environment, they are bad for business and the future of industry as well. Tourist developments are pointless if they destroy or pollute the beautiful coasts where they are located. Fisheries are pointless if overfishing destroys future fish stocks.

The debate about our changing coastal regions is not limited to idealists or dreamers. It is about common sense and survival.

Beaches can become polluted if they are not carefully managed.

Coastal pollution
Overcrowding
Water supplies limited

Environmental damage

Fewer tourists

Government spends money on clean-up

GLOSSARY

Accretion A gathering together or growth.

Atmosphere The gases that surround Earth.

Atoll A ring of coral reefs or islands surrounding a lagoon.

Barrage A barrier aross a river mouth, especially one used to generate power.

Barrier reef A coral reef that runs parallel to a coastline or rings an island.

Blow hole A hole eroded in the roof of a sea cave through which air and water are forced whenever a wave comes in.

Breakwater A structure designed to break the force of waves or currents.

Conservation The protection and care (of the environment).

Continental drift The slow movement of the plates that support the world's landmasses.

Continental shelf The underwater edge of a continent lying beneath shallow seas.

Crust The outermost layer of the rocks which make up the planet.

Delta The plain formed by sediment at a river mouth that forces the river to split into separate channels.

Dislocation The displacement of rock around a fault.

Dredge To scoop out sediment from a river or seabed dike.

Erosion The wearing down of a landscape by natural forces, such as wind and waves.

Estuary A river mouth.

Fjord A deep sea inlet created by the flooding of a glacial valley (also, fiord).

Friction The rubbing of one surface against another.

Fringing reef A platform of coral extending from the coast out to sea.

Global warming A rise in the average temperatures experienced on Earth.

Groyne A barrier extending from the shore to reduce currents and hinder erosion.

Habitat The environment in which a species of plant or animal can thrive.

Hotspot A weak point in the Earth's crust where magma can break through.

Hurricane A severe tropical storm, also known as a cyclone or a typhoon.

Lagoon A shallow, calm area of water protected from the open sea by mudbanks or coral reefs.

Landmass One of the world's major areas of dry land, such as Eurasia (made up of Europe and Asia).

Lava The red-hot, molten rock that bursts out of a volcano.

Magma The molten rock beneath Earth's crust.

Mantle The layer of rock between Earth's crust and its core.

Mollusk One of a group of soft-bodied creatures, many with external shells.

Pack ice	A mass of ice floes that become packed together.
Plate	A section of Earth's crust.
Polder	Land reclaimed from the sea.
Raised beach	A beach left high and dry as a result of falling sea levels or geological movement.
Reclaim	To take back land from the sea.
Reef	A platform or ridge of rock or coral lying at or near the surface of the sea.
Renewable energy	A means of producing electricity that does not use up fuel, such as power from wind, sun, or tides.
Salt marsh	A mudflat beside a coast or estuary which is sometimes flooded by the sea.
Sediment	Rock or other matter that has been worn down into sand or mud and carried along by rivers or ocean currents.
Sedimentary rock	Rock formed from sediment that has built up on the ocean floor and been compressed.
Silt	A fine, muddy sediment.
Stack	An offshore pillar of rock or small island that has been separated from cliffs by erosion.
Water table	The level at which rocks become saturated.

FURTHER INFORMATION

U.S. Environmental Protection Agency
Information on programs to protect oceans, coasts, and estuaries in the United States.

www.epa.gov/owow/oceans/

United States Coral Reef Task Force
Provides information on U.S. coral reefs, along with strategies to preserve coral reef habitats worldwide.

www.coralreef.gov

Mississippi River Delta Basin
A guide to the Mississippi River Basin and its effect on the coastline of Louisiana.

http://www.lacoast.gov/cwppra/projects/mississippi/

Center for the Study of Carbon Dioxide and Global Change
An organization dedicated to studying the effect of carbon dioxide on global climate.

http://www.co2science.org/center.htm

Greenpeace
A global organization that works to protect the planet's biodiversity and environment.

www.greenpeace.org

Friends of the Earth International
A coalition of worldwide environmental groups with information on changes to coastlines.

www.foei.org

INDEX